GOD'S BLUEPRINT FOR MARRIAGE

A How-to Guide for

Godly Marriage

Relationship

JIM & MARSHA DIXON

GOD'S BLUEPRINT FOR MARRIAGE

A How-to Guide for

Godly Marriage

Relationship

First Edition

Unless otherwise noted, all Scripture quotations are from the NEW AMERICAN STANDARD BIBLE®, Copyright © 1960,1962,1963,1968,1971,1972,1973,1975,1977,1995 by The Lockman Foundation. Used by permission.

God's Blueprint for Marriage
© 2013 by Jim and Marsha Dixon
www.godsblueprintformarriage.com
Email: jimd@godsblueprint.info

ISBN: 978-1500919894

DEDICATION

There could be no other than Jesus Christ to whom we could dedicate this book. Without Him there is no way of knowing where we would be today. Likely we would no longer be married to one another, living a life full of disappointment.   He intervened at a time when we thought our marriage was over.

To God be the glory forever and ever. Amen

CONTENTS

1

FORWARD

It is quite true that the concept of marriage was made in heaven, but marriage itself has to be worked out on earth. The concept is flawless; the working out is rife with potential problems and pitfalls, as too many men and women have experienced.

As a marriage and family therapist, working primarily with Christian couples, it never ceases to amaze me how easy it is to mess up the wonderful and seemingly simple plan of God. The good intentions, hopes and dreams of a couple entering in to what is, by design, to be a life time journey of companionship often turns into a battle for power or control, driven by selfishness and immaturity.

God's Blue Print for Marriage is both theological and practical. Set in the story of a very dysfunctional marriage (the Dixon's), Jim and Marsha share, in a unique and engaging style, principles for the Word of God and common sense to help couples, from the radically dysfunctional to those who want to strengthen an existing strong marriage, to have healthy, happy and successful relationships that will last.

Traditional marriage and family life in America has been under attack for more than a generation, eroding the sanctity of marriage vows, and cheapening the value of covenant in marriage. Young people have been under a near constant assault to compromise values such as chastity and faithfulness in relationship. Broken relationships in the world become the problem of the church as people seek help from the one and only truly stable and effective restoring institution of the day....the church of Jesus Christ. In spite of the attack on traditional marriage and a biblical view of marriage, thousands are seeking the message of hope found in the gospel of Christ, and the guidance from the ancient words of the Bible. This book, written by two people who have experienced the best and worst of marriage life, is an excellent help for those seeking God's wisdom.

Stan E. DeKoven, Ph.D., MFT
Founder and President
Vision International University

PREFACE

Look in the library or at the bookstore and you'll find myriads of books on marriage. So, what makes this one different?

Most marriage books are written by psychologists, counselors or other professionals who base their writings on research, case studies and their own philosophical ideas. This book, on the other hand, is born out of our own personal experiences.

What we share here is our own story, and how God brought us through the turmoil of a bad marriage into a marriage that, we hope, is a model for others.

To be a marriage model is an awesome responsibility, because a biblical marriage is a reflection of the relationship between Christ and His bride, the church. For some, that model may be the only such representation they will ever see. Our hope is that we can not only be that model, but help others become that model as well.

Some marriage experts may find areas of disagreement with us. That's okay because this is not intended to be a scholarly textbook, but a how-to manual. And, if you approach it as such, you will not only read, but also apply the teaching we share.

Of one thing we are certain. God walked us through the restoration process at a time when others, including "Christian counselors", told us to give up.

If your marriage is struggling, we suggest you approach your problems in three steps: 1) Repentance; 2) Reconciliation; and 3) Restoration. Though repentance and reconciliation are addressed, the focus is on what we learned in the restoration process, and how applying those things will make a difference.

If you are not yet married, this book will give you helpful insights in preparing for a godly marriage. If you have a good marriage, this book will help you make it better. And if, like we were, your marriage is in trouble, this book will help you become the godly couple the Lord intends for you to be.

We encourage you to read this book prayerfully, asking God to speak to you through its pages. And as you do, we are praying, too, that God will give you just what your need at this point in your marriage.

If you have questions or comments, please feel free to share them. Jim's email address is *jimd@godsblueprint.info*. Marsha's is *marsha@godsblueprint.info*. May God richly bless you as you read.

ACKNOWLEDGEMENTS

So many have influenced us in the restoration of our marriage, and the writing of this book. Those include Dr. Larry Lea, who taught us how prayer could have such a dramatic impact on our lives. Also, Bishop Gary McIntosh, who first told us that the Lord wanted us to write. Our sons, Mike and Jeff, who kept encouraging us (or egging us on) to finish the book.

One who had a direct hand in the restoration process —though he was not aware of it— was Dr. James Dobson and Focus on the Family. We had escaped to Dallas shortly after reconciling, still questioning whether things would work out between us. While on that trip we listened to a Focus broadcast and, though we couldn't tell you, now, what the program was about, that program was the final word that gave us the hope we needed to continue.

We also want to thank Dr. Stan DeKoven, founder and President of Vision International University, for his help in proofing and suggested changes made to the final draft, and for his encouraging words in the Forward of this book.

PART ONE

CHAPTER ONE
NOBODY BUT JESUS...

It was not a healthy marriage; it had not been for fifteen years. Jim was singularly focused on his career, to the point that he said to his wife, Marsha, "Don't put me in a position of having to choose between you and my career, because you will lose."

Marsha accused him, saying, "If I file for divorce, I'll name your career as the correspondent in the case, because you are having an affair with it."

There were long, lonely nights, when Jim was away at work. But fortunately, they both thought, their close friend, who had lived with them off and on for several years, was there to keep her company.

Marsha didn't intend for the friendship to develop into an affair; it just happened. And it continued for nine years. Jim never knew. But they say the husband is always the last to know.

In the meantime, Jim was actively pursuing his career that wasn't just his mistress; it was his god. But one day his career came to a crashing halt. And his god was dead. And for the next year he drifted in and out of depression, working at a job he hated.

A little more than a year passed, and Jim knew something had to change. He read a long list of self-help books, thinking he could "find himself" and become successful again. But nothing seemed to work. In the meantime, Jim and Marsha lost everything— their home, their car, their self-esteem. They were just barely getting by.

Sitting in their living room one evening, Jim said to Marsha, "I know somebody who can help me get through this." Jim called a friend who had undergone a dramatic change in his own life after finding a relationship with Jesus Christ. That night, in his friend's home, Jim gave his life to the Lord.

Meanwhile, Marsha had been reading Anne Ortlund's book, Disciplines of the Beautiful Woman[1]. And just two days before Jim gave his life to the Lord, Marsha bowed her head and prayed, "Lord, I know there must be more. Whatever you have for me, Lord, I want it." And she gave her life to Christ.

Jim and Marsha had both become Christians, but nothing in their relationship with each other changed. And neither did Marsha's

11

relationship with "the other man". But because she had invited Jesus into her life, He took up residence, and His Holy Spirit began to work on her, convicting her of the sin in her life. She eventually ended the affair physically, but not emotionally. And she was eaten up with guilt, experiencing nightmares, hearing voices and waking up screaming. The voices were telling her that if God were real, He would take away the nightmares. Marsha entered a deep depression and decided to take her own life. Placing a loaded Smith & Wesson .357 magnum revolver in her mouth, she pulled the trigger.

The gun failed to fire. God had divinely intervened. In an audible voice Marsha heard the words, "Who do you think you are! You have no right! You belong to Me."

The depression immediately lifted and the nightmares ceased. But the conviction continued.

It was some years later that Marsha sensed the depression returning. She confessed her sin to their pastor. His advice was to not tell Jim because of "the male ego." Her visit with the pastor did not help the depression.

One Wednesday evening, Marsha shared with Jim her disappointment that their "friend", who had promised to be at the evening church service, failed to show up. Jim asked Marsha why she was so disappointed. She tried to "spiritualize" her answer, but Jim sensed there was more to it. For the first time, he suspected that Marsha's relationship with their "friend" was deeper than he had realized.

Jim asked Marsha if she had been sleeping with their friend. Everything inside of Marsha told her to say, "No." But she found herself saying, "Yes," instead.

In one way, Jim was glad. Some years before, Jim asked God if he could leave Marsha and file for divorce. He sensed God saying to him, "The price you'd have to pay is greater than you'd be willing to pay." But now he was no longer bound to the marriage. Marsha had given him biblical grounds for divorce. Yet, at that moment, he felt as though his heart had been ripped from his chest. His wife and his most trusted friend...right under his nose. And he never knew.

Following her confession, Marsha disappeared. Jim called their pastor, who came over immediately. While the pastor was on the way, Jim took everything in the house that belonged to their "friend", and threw it into a pile in the front yard.   Upon the pastor's arrival, thinking Marsha had left, Jim and the pastor went looking for her. It was then that Jim slammed his hand on the top of the pastor's car and said, "Nobody but Jesus is going to have my wife."

A short time later they found Marsha. She had never left the house, but was sitting on the patio, pondering what was next. She was afraid she was going to lose everything, especially their two sons. After all, she thought, she was the one in the wrong. So she would be the one to pay the greater price.

The next day, the two of them sat down to "split the sheets"—decide how to separate, divide the assets, and for each to start over. There were the children to consider.   In the midst of their discussion, Marsha said, "I know God has forgiven me, but how do I forgive myself?"

Amazingly, Jim was able to reply in a way that answered Marsha's question. Going to the Gospel of John, chapter 8, Jim read the story.

> 1 But Jesus went to the Mount of Olives.
> 2 And early in the morning He came

again into the temple, and all the people were coming to Him; and He sat down and began to teach them. 3 And the scribes and the Pharisees brought a woman caught in adultery, and having set her in the midst, 4 they said to Him, "Teacher, this woman has been caught in adultery, in the very act. 5 "Now in the Law Moses commanded us to stone such women; what then do You say?" 6 And they were saying this, testing Him, in order that they might have grounds for accusing Him. But Jesus stooped down, and with His finger wrote on the ground. 7 But when they persisted in asking Him, He straightened up, and said to them, "He who is without sin among you, let him be the first to throw a stone at her." 8 And again He stooped down, and wrote on the ground. 9 And when they heard it, they began to go out one by one, beginning with the older ones, and He was left alone, and the woman, where she was, in the midst. 10 And straightening up, Jesus said to her, "Woman, where are they? Did no one condemn you?" 11 And she said, "No one, Lord." And Jesus said, "Neither do I condemn you; go your way. From now on sin no more."

Jim said to Marsha, "If God has forgiven you and you don't forgive yourself, you are placing yourself above God." It was at that point Jim heard a voice ask him "So what makes you so different?" With that revelation, Jim was able to completely forgive Marsha. But he still had to deal with his own failure in the marriage.

Jim told Marsha, "Jesus gave the adulteress woman a fresh start. And He is giving you one, too." Something "clicked" inside of Marsha. She realized that God had set her free, not only from the bondage of her sin, but also the guilt. For the first time she was right with God and nothing else mattered, even if she lost her husband, sons and home. She was truly free.

But God was not through with them that day. The two of them looked at each other as though they had never seen one another before, and fell deeply, madly in love with each other. Jim asked Marsha to forgive him for creating the vacuum in her life that led to the affair. She asked him to forgive her for the affair.

Jim wanted to make it clear that he was cancelling his right to divorce. He wanted to start over with a clean slate. He asked Marsha to marry him, and she said yes.

That night Jim and Marsha renewed their marriage covenant. And from that time on, it was as though her nine year affair with the other man and his fifteen year affair with his career had never happened. And they set out on a brand new journey together, knowing what it was like to truly be in love.

This book shares the things that brought us beyond reconciliation to restoration. Reconciliation was immediate, but restoration was a process. In that process God revealed to us the principles of His Blueprint for Marriage. Learn these principles and apply them to your own marriage. If you have a bad marriage, these principles will help you turn it into a good marriage. And if you have a good marriage, these principles will make it even better.

[1] Anne Ortuland, *Disciplines of the Beautiful Woman* (Word, Inc., Waco Texas, 1981)

CHAPTER TWO
WHEN YOU PRAY...GOD'S CHARACTER

MARSHA: Before Jim and I were married, I thought the only thing we needed to make a good marriage was our love for each other. But love cannot carry you in the bad times; only Jesus can. And, when we were first married, we did not have Jesus in our lives. Later, when I realized we had a bad marriage, I didn't know what we could do about it. I bought books and books and books. I read all the magazine articles on marriage. Then I gave them to Jim to read. I was looking for the answer to our bad marriage in these books and magazine articles. I also knew that the problem was not me! I knew that the reason for our bad marriage was Jim.

JIM: *And I knew that Marsha was the problem. She wasn't the person I thought she was. And it wasn't a fairy tale marriage. Then in August of 1980, we both had an encounter with Jesus Christ.*
When you meet Jesus it changes your perspective. We learned that there really were some good marriages out there--Christ-centered marriages. Some people who said they had a good marriage were not lying after all.

Just meeting Jesus didn't solve our marriage problems, but it did change our perspective about marriage.

MARSHA: After becoming Christians we looked at everything differently, especially our marriage. We knew we had a major problem. As we read and studied the word of God we realized that as Christians, divorce was not an option. So we decided in 1980 to take the word "divorce" out of our vocabulary, out of our dictionary, and out of our thinking.

You have two alternatives when you have a bad marriage. You can either live with the bad marriage, or you can do something to change it. But we still did not know what to do about our bad marriage.

JIM: *For those who are divorced and remarried, this is not about your previous marriage, but about your present marriage. When you receive Christ as your savior the past is forgiven. As Marsha shared, we had two options: 1) to either continue living in a bad marriage, which was not a real exciting idea; or 2)work toward making a good marriage. And one thing we learned in a hurry is that those books were not working.*

19

MARSHA: Jim wouldn't read them! He thought that when I gave him those books, I was pointing my finger at him (which I probably was.) He didn't realize that before I gave him those books I read them first. Like most "How to" books, they had a few good words of counsel, but for me they did not work, or I did not know how to make them work.

JIM: *We have read the books again since then and we have picked up a lot of principles. But at the time, I did not want to hear it…especially the parts she wanted me to hear. Besides, I didn't need to change. I wasn't the problem! I didn't know why she kept giving me all this stuff when she was the problem. So, I began looking for other solutions.*

Many times in our lives we decide that prayer might lead us to the answer. So I started praying for Marsha, something like, "Oh God, change Marsha into the woman I need. Change her Oh God." I was diligent in my prayers for her but was, without realizing it, trying to do the Holy Spirit's work. I wanted Him to make her see her need to change. At the same time I was unknowingly trying to be her Holy Spirit, she was trying to be mine.

Then, in 1986, I heard a series of messages by Dr. Larry Lea on the Lord's Prayer as a 6-point outline.[2] I learned to pray, "Our Father who art in heaven, hallowed be Thy name," and that when I was hallowing the name of God I was honoring His character. I was also acknowledging that all of the characteristics—the character and nature of God—are revealed in the life of one Man, Jesus Christ. And I also realized that my objective as a Christian was to become like Jesus. And so, as I was praying for God's character and nature to be revealed to me and to be established in me, I began to change.

I began to pray, "Hallowed be Thy name Jehovah-Tsidkenu—Jehovah God my righteousness (Jer 33:16)".—You are my righteousness, and I want to be like You, and I want Your righteousness in me." And as I began to pray, "God, put your righteousness in me," He began to put His righteousness in me!

I prayed, "Hallowed be Thy Name, Jehovah M'Kaddesh, God who sanctifies (Lev 20:8)." I was praying, "God sanctify me by Your Holy Spirit." When you see all of these attributes of Jesus fulfilled through the covenant names of God in your lives, it will change your life. It did mine.

21

I prayed "Hallowed be Thy Name, Jehovah Shammah, God Who is ever present (Ezekiel 48:35)." And I sensed a greater depth of the presence of God in my life. And being in the presence of God will change you…it certainly changed me. The more time I spent in His presence, the more I realized I was being transformed as my mind was renewed (Romans 12:1,2)

I prayed, "Hallowed be Thy Name, Jehovah-Shalom, the God of Peace (Judges 6:24)". Though there was no peace in our marriage at the time I began praying, I found His peace began to penetrate my heart. And as it did, it began to penetrate my home also.

I prayed, "Hallowed by Thy Name, Jehovah-Jireh, God whose provision shall be seen (Gen 22:14)." One of the struggles we had faced during our years of marriage turmoil was finances. In our years of pastoral counseling, we have found many marriage problems were related to money or sex. In lots of cases, we saw that the sex problems were diminished when finance problems were addressed and corrections made. (We will have more to say about that in a later chapter.)

In our own situation, we were having a "lively discussion". (If you had been listening, you might have called it a heated exchange. However, we weren't yelling at each other...we were just being "emphatic"!) The topic of our "discussion" was finances. Marsha asked, "What are we going to do about it?" My response was "I don't know what we're going to do about it!" At that moment I looked at the end table by my chair in the living room. There on the table was a Phillips translation of the Bible, open to Romans 8:18. Above the verse, as a headline to the text, were these words, "Present distress is temporary and negligible." The verse below read, "In my opinion, whatever we have to go through is next to nothing compared to the magnificent future God has in store for us." As I read those words aloud, the realization came that God was in total control of every area of our lives, including our finances. And something broke at that moment. Hallowing God's Name as our Provider began to have real meaning for us.

I prayed, "Hallowed be Thy Name, Jehovah-Rapha, the God Who heals." (Exodus15;25-26)

I thanked Him for the healing experiences we had experienced in the past. Marsha had

23

been diagnosed with advanced cervical cancer a few years before, and had been told by her doctor to "go home and get your affairs in order." He gave her no hope for survival. A friend of ours in another city was a Christian whose church had an active prayer chain. The friend asked Marsha if she would like to have the prayer chain pray for her. Though we were not Christians at the time, we did believe in the power of prayer, and thought "It couldn't hurt anything, and it might actually help." The people in that church prayed constantly for Marsha, twenty-four hours a day for the next several days. The following week Marsha's doctor examined her to see how much farther the cancer had advanced. But, to his surprise—and ours—there was no sign of cancer! Marsha had been completely healed! We had experienced the power of Jehovah-Rapha even before we knew Him.

We had many more encounters with the healing power of God, including an x-ray documented healing of stomach ulcers that I had been suffering with for some time. But it was in 1995 that we saw His power at work in Marsha once again. We were in New Hampshire to do a cell leader training workshop, when Marsha began to suffer from severe migraine headaches. They would strike about every other day, each one with increased severity. After returning home to Oklahoma she awoke during the night with pain so intense we went to the hospital emergency room where she was given a shot of Demerol and a prescription for pain pills. A day or two later she had another headache, and I took her a pain pill. She looked at me and said, with slurred speech, "I don't remember...." I couldn't figure out what she couldn't remember, and she couldn't tell me. Finally, it dawned on me...she couldn't remember how to take a pill! She finally managed to get the pill down and went to sleep, and I went to my office at the church.

Later that day, I was in a staff meeting when the church secretary interrupted to tell me that Marsha was on the phone. I asked her to tell Marsha that I was in a meeting and would call her back. The secretary's response was, "I think you need to take this call."

When I answered, Marsha told me that the garage door wouldn't open. I could tell by the tone in her voice there was more going on that just a faulty garage door opener, so I rushed home, arriving to find the garage door closed and the car inside running...not a good sign. I moved to turn the engine off, only to find the car locked.

That particular model car had a safety feature preventing locking the door from the outside with the engine running. It could only be locked from the <u>inside</u>, prompting us to later ask, "Who locked the car?" Our conclusion: knowing it could only be locked from the inside, God had to have sent an angel to lock the door and prevent Marsha from trying to leave.

I found my keyless entry to the car and unlocked the door, turned off the ignition and removed the keys. I then went inside to find Marsha, in a dress, heels and hose. The vacuum sweeper was in the middle of the living room with the cord still wrapped around the handle. Marsha explained that she had tried to vacuum the floor, but the sweeper wouldn't work. She didn't realize that the sweeper had to be plugged in. She told me she also tried to mow the lawn (still in heels and hose) while waiting for me to come home, but the lawn mower wouldn't work, either. She did not remember you had to pull the starter rope to make it run.

Marsha continued a downward mental spiral. She became irrational. She could not make decisions involving two choices. For example, you could ask her if she wanted a Coke and she could answer "yes" or "no". But if you asked her if she wanted a Coke or 7-Up, she would go into gridlock, unable to respond. If you asked her what her phone number was, she could tell you. But if you handed her a telephone and asked her to call the number, she would, again, gridlock.

After three days in the hospital, where no cause for Marsha's illness could be diagnosed, she was sent home, where family and church members assisted me in taking care of her, since she could no longer care for herself. We waited word from the Mayo Clinic in Rochester, Minnesota, where her neurologist had referred her for diagnosis and treatment. In the meantime, the doctors in Tulsa told us to prepare for the worst...this could be a potentially fatal illness.

Finally, the call came, and we took her to the Mayo Clinic, where it was determined that she had a rare viral disease that was destroying her brain cells. The neurologist at the clinic told us that most people who suffer from the disease never recover, but wind up permanently disabled.

However, Marsha was already beginning to show signs of recovery. Before leaving for Rochester she could not sign her name. But she was so proud of herself to have signed

27

herself in to the laboratory where tests were to be performed to confirm the doctor's diagnosis.

Though it took her a year to fully recover from the illness, she was restored to health, to the amazement of many physicians who said she would be permanently mentally disabled. But we knew the Great Physician, Jehovah-Rapha, God who Heals!

I prayed, "Hallowed be Thy Name, Jehovah-Nissi, God my Banner." The banner referred to in this context is a "battle-standard", like the soldiers carried to identify their unit. Or, perhaps the best example is the Marines raising the American flag in the battle at Iwo Jima during World War Two. That event not only became a rallying point for that battle, but continues today to serve as an example of how the banner rallies the army. As long as they see the banner, they know they're still in the fight. "God my Banner" is like that flag. It represents the ultimate victory we have through Christ.

And, I prayed, "Hallowed be Thy Name, Jehovah-Rohi, God my Shepherd (Psalm 23)." We are described in the Bible as "like sheep". And sheep need a shepherd. When I prayed "God my Shepherd", I recalled the Twenty-

Third Psalm, "The Lord is My Shepherd; I shall not want..." (Psalm 23) As my Shepherd, God guides, provides, protects, nurtures...

As I hallowed God's Name, recognizing His character as revealed in the covenant names, I was acknowledging that His character was revealed in its totality in the Person of Jesus. And, as I saw His character revealed, I longed to be like Him, having His character established in my life.

We are to look to Christ as our example, and in following Him, strive to be like Him. That's what was taking place in my life...I was striving to become like Jesus. And, slowly, my character was changing as I was being conformed in His image. "For whom He foreknew, He also predestined to become conformed to the image of His Son... " Romans 8:29) God was changing me!

[2]Larry Lea, *Could You Not Tarry One Hour?* (Creation House, Strang Communications Company, Altamonte Springs, Florida, 1987)

CHAPTER THREE
ESTABLISHING THE KINGDOM

The next verse in the Lord's Prayer says, "Thy Kingdom Come, Thy will be done, on earth as it is in Heaven (Matt 6:10)." Literally translated, that phrase is, "Come Kingdom, Be done, Will of God." It's not a request, but a declarative faith statement.

And as I began to pray, "Come kingdom of God, be done will of God in my life," establishing His character and nature in my own life, I was also establishing His will in my life as well.

I then realized I can't pray, "God, change Marsha," until I am willing to first pray, "God, change me." If I'm not willing to let God change me, I am hindering the flow of God's love, grace and mercy as He flows through me, as the head of the house, down into the family. My prayers were out of order when I was praying, "God, change Marsha." But when I began to start praying, "God, change me", I opened the channel to allow the Holy Spirit to come and change me and flow downward to Marsha.

Then I could pray, "Come kingdom of God; be done will of God in my wife's life." It was no longer the "God, change Marsha" prayer that I had been praying, but I something like, "Lord Jesus, rule and reign without rival in Marsha's heart." And I would declare by faith, "Nobody but Jesus is going to rule my wife." For more than twenty-five years I am still praying that the Lord Jesus would rule and reign without rival in Marsha's heart." As I prayed these prayers, something happened because I had opened the door for God to move in me and change me.

MARSHA: When the series on the Lord's Prayer was taught at our church, I did not attend, But a short time after Jim began praying the Lord's Prayer, the Holy Spirit began working in me, and my prayers changed. Instead of praying, "Lord please, whatever You do, change Jim. Make him what I need," I began to pray, "Lord, change me. Help me, Lord, to be all that he needs in a wife and a helpmate."

I can't say that something miraculously happened overnight. I just continually prayed, "Lord, change me. Soften me; help me to be what Jim needs." It was an awakening that God really was changing me from the inside out. He changed my heart.

I believe He also changed my eyesight. I looked at Jim in a totally different way. I saw him through the eyes of Jesus. He wasn't the bad person—the miserable husband or father that I thought he was. I began seeing him as a creation of Jesus and that he meant everything to Jesus. I began seeing the qualities Jim had, and the possibilities. And if I would allow them in my heart, I would see that Jim wasn't the creep that I thought he was.

JIM: *There are many times that couples prevent God from pouring into their marriage because one mate is standing between God and the other, blocking the flow. (We will share more about that in a coming chapter.) Wives will often try to shape and mold their husbands into the image they want. I know because I had a wife like that.*

And husbands, we're just as guilty. We try to shape and mold our wives into the image we want.

How you pray for yourself and for your wife will determine the flow of God's blessing into your marriage. If you are praying, "God, change her," It is not going to happen. But when you pray, "God, change me," it's amazing how much change will take place! As I prayed, "God change me," Marsha began to change. But it wasn't so much that she changed, but my perspective of her changed and I changed.

When we started praying this way our marriage was at an all-time low. Praying this way opened the door of opportunity for God to work in our hearts.

CHAPTER FOUR
READY TO SPLIT THE SHEETS!

MARSHA: We were about 60 seconds away from ending the marriage. When I revealed my affair to Jim, it was a nightmare. I knew our marriage was over. I thought, "What are we going to do. Who's going to get what? What are we going to do with the boys? Where am I going to go? Am I going to stay? Is he going to go?"

We had been living together as male and female but not as man and wife. We were just roommates sharing the same bed. He had his life and I had mine. He went his way and I went mine.

JIM: A critical battle was being fought that night when I slammed my fist on the top of our pastor's car, pointed my boney finger at him and said, "Nobody but Jesus is going to have my wife." That was the turning point.

The next day, as we were sitting down to discuss how we were going to "split the sheets" (divide our assets), I looked at Marsha and, for the first time, really fell in love with

*her. Suddenly, I knew I could not live without
her. God had changed me!*

*MARSHA: And He had changed me. I looked
at Jim and realized that he was the man I
wanted to spend the rest of my life with.*

*JIM: What had happened? It began with a
prayer that included, "God, I want to be like
You. I ask You to establish Your character in
my life." And it also included, "God, change
me. Nobody but Jesus is going to rule and
reign in my heart." And, "Nobody but Jesus is
going to rule and reign in my wife's heart."*

CHAPTER FIVE
OUR SOURCE

As we continue our look at the Lord's Prayer, we come to the line that says,, "Give us this day, our daily bread."³ Your job is not your source; your mate's job is not your source. God is your source. He is Jehovah-Jireh, your Provider. Many anxious moments about provision can create conflict between husband and wife. But when you realize that He is your source of supply, and you look to Him and not to each other, peace can settle into your hearts.

Some of our biggest battles have been over finances. In a previous chapter I shared how we were having one of our "discussions" (you might have called it an argument, but we were each just being emphatic!) I looked down at a Phillips Translation of the New Testament, opened to Romans 8. Those words just above verse 18, the words: "Present distress is temporary and negligible." Those words that followed, "In my opinion, whatever we have to go through is less than nothing compared to the magnificent future God has in store for us," spoke an immediate release of the pressure we were feeling. We both knew that the outcome was secured by our Savior.

Things didn't get better immediately; in fact circumstances grew worse for a time. But we knew that those circumstances were "temporary and negligible".

The Lord's Prayer says, "Give us <u>today</u>…" Most of our anxious moments are about <u>tomorrow's</u> needs. As we learn to trust <u>God day-by-day</u>, we learn that day-by-day He will meet our needs.

Throughout the scriptures God reveals Himself as our source. When Moses led the children of Israel out of Egypt, God provided food and water as they traveled through the wilderness.

In Psalm 37:25, David writes about how he has "never seen the righteous forsaken, or his seed begging for bread."

In the Sermon on the Mount, Jesus tells us to seek first His kingdom and His righteousness, and all these things (our needs) will be added to us.[5]

Paul, in his letter to the Philippian church, commended the church for their faithfulness in giving, and told them because of their faithfulness, that God would supply all their needs. [6] It's just as true today.

Our problem is we don't want to wait for God to provide, so we make our own arrangements for provision. We get caught up in a world of credit, and find ourselves drowning in a sea of debt. We've heard it all—and said it ourselves! "We only use our credit card for emergencies." It's as though we are saying, "In God we trust, except in emergencies. Then we trust MasterCard."

It is amazing what will constitute an emergency. Initially it might be a blown tire that has to be replaced before you go on a trip. But, sooner or later, it becomes a need for a new pair of pants to wear to the party. Or a dinner you really can't afford, but you justify as an "emergency" because you and your mate need a night out.

Giving…stewardship…faith…trust…all these come into play when trusting God for our daily bread. The bottom line is this: God, our heavenly Father, wants to provide for us. What He expects from us in response to His willingness is to love Him with all of our heart, and all of our mind, and all of our strength. "Seek first the kingdom of God."[5]

So, a couple needs to ask God, daily, for daily bread, not being anxious about tomorrow's bread, but in gratitude receiving provision for today.

[3]Matthew 6:11

J. B. Phillips, "The New Testament in Modern English", 1962 edition by HarperCollins

[5]Matthew 8:33

[6]Philippians 4:19

CHAPTER SIX
BUT THE RECIPE SAID TOMATO SAUCE!

Jesus told His followers to pray, "Forgive us our debts, as we also have forgiven our debtors."[7] One of the biggest marriage killers is unforgiveness. The wife says or does something, and the husband is offended by it. Or the husband says or does something and the wife is offended. Either way, the result is the same. And an offense is like a brick. Each single offense, by itself, does not build a wall of separation between a husband and a wife. But brick by brick, offense by offense, a wall is built, and that wall, once built, is difficult to tear down. So it was with Marsha and me. Offense by offense, brick by brick, we had built a wall between us.

And it's been true in every marriage counseling session we have conducted. It begins with one saying of the other, "He always does this...", or "She always does that..."

As Jesus hung on the cross, He said, "Father, forgive them for they don't know what they are doing (Luke 23:34)." He wasn't just talking about those that had gathered around Him,

*crucifying Him. He was looking across the
expanse of time, talking to you and me. He
was talking as if **we** had been there ourselves,
driving the nails into His hands and feet. It
was our sin that put Jesus Christ on the cross.
And as He hung there and said, "Father
forgive them ...", He was forgiving me before I
ever committed my first offense against Him.*

*If I am praying to establish Jesus' character
and nature in my own life, how can I do any
less? When I pray "Forgive us our debts as
we forgive our debtors," I have already
chosen to forgive the offense before it comes,
just as He already chose to forgive the offense
before it came 2000 years ago. I have
purposed in my heart that there is nothing
anyone can do to offend me. Marsha cannot
offend me because I have already purposed in
my heart not to be offended.*

*That might sound self-righteous. It is not that I
don't get offended; but I have made a choice.
I have purposed in my heart, with the help of
the Holy Spirit, not to be offended. Therefore,
when I start getting offended, He brings
conviction and correction .*

*Here's an example of how this works. A
couple was coming to our home for premarital
counseling. It was their last session with us,*

*and our custom was to invite them to share an evening meal with us after that last session. We were having spaghetti and meat sauce that evening, and Marsha called to ask me to stop at the grocery store on the way home and buy tomato sauce. But I bought tomato **paste** by mistake.*

MARSHA: And I'm one of those that follows the recipe. If it says one teaspoon, I use one teaspoon. I don't ad lib a recipe. I use just exactly what it calls for. And my recipe called for tomato **sauce**.

*JIM: When I arrived home with tomato **paste**, Marsha informed me emphatically, that she said tomato **sauce**. I told her that if you add water to tomato paste you have tomato sauce. I added that everybody should know that!*

MARSHA: But the recipe called for tomato sauce!!!!!!!!

JIM: And I told her, again, just to add water and she would have tomato sauce. She told me, no, she needed tomato sauce. So, we locked horns, and she got in the car to go buy tomato sauce.

MARSHA: And on the way to the grocery store I met the couple coming to our house.

JIM: *Here we are, minutes away from a premarital counseling session, and we're at odds with each other. The devil is so tricky. Of all things in the world to hamper a premarital counseling session…a can of tomato sauce!*

While Marsha was on her way to the grocery store, I realized I had taken offense over her refusing to use the can of tomato paste as a substitute for tomato sauce. Because I had already prayed, "Lord, I choose to be a forgiver before the offense ever occurs," my prayer opened the door for the Holy Spirit to convict me of the offense.

When Marsha returned from the grocery store, before we met with the couple I asked her to forgive me for not buying tomato sauce instead of tomato paste. She, in turn, asked me to forgive her for blowing up over it. We prayed together, and then joined the couple waiting in the living room to begin their final session of premarital counseling.

Not wanting to waste an opportunity for an illustration, I shared with the couple what just happened. When I said, "I bought tomato paste instead of tomato sauce," the woman we were counseling said, "Well Marsha, all you had to do was add water to the tomato paste and you would have had tomato sauce!"

So now when I go to the store and she asks for tomato sauce I buy a can of each just in case.

Jesus said, "For if you forgive men for their transgressions, your heavenly Father will also forgive you. "But if you do not forgive men, then your Father will not forgive your transgressions" (Matt 6:14-15).

Every marriage counseling session we have held is over offense. Marsha and I have resolved that we are not going to be offended by each other. It's a decision we came to the realization that offense is a choice.

[7]Matthew 6:12

CHAPTER SEVEN
And Lead us Not Into Temptation

Jesus' final instruction on prayer was, "And lead us not into temptation, but deliver us from evil (Matt 6:13)."

The best way to not yield to temptation is to avoid it altogether. Paul instructed his son in the faith, Timothy, to "flee youthful lusts (2 Tim 2:22). Seldom does one win by taking temptation head on, thinking they are strong enough to endure in the face of that temptation.

One of the greatest temptations one faces is sexual temptation. That's why boundaries— rules—should be set in advance. Otherwise, here's what might happen:

> *John and Susan work together at a major corporation. They have been working on a major project, and the deadline looms near. As lunch approached, John said to Susan, "We've got to finish today, but I'm starving. Let's grab our stuff and go work over lunch." Susan agreed, and they worked through lunch together, meeting the deadline.*

A couple weeks later, John passed by Susan's desk and complimented her on her dress. Susan thanked him as John moved on toward his own desk. Susan found herself thinking, "My husband didn't notice my new dress. It was nice of John to say something."

Sometime later, John's wife and Susan's husband were both out of town. John said to Susan, "I hate to eat alone. Why don't we meet at the Downtown Café and have dinner before heading home?" It was an honest invitation. They had become close friends and, after all, there's nothing wrong with friends having dinner together. They both enjoyed the meal, and afterwards both went their own way.

The following week, as John walked by Susan's desk, he commented, "You smell nice today. That's a different perfume than you normally wear, isn't it?" As he walked away, Susan thinks, "My husband never says anything about my perfume."

It wasn't too long after that, Susan's husband was out of town again. Knowing John's wife was gone also, Susan suggested they go to a movie they both had wanted to see but that their spouses were not interested in. They agreed and met at the theater, sat together and shared popcorn and enjoyed the movie. After all, there's nothing wrong with good friends spending the evening together.

Some time passed, and again both of their spouses were out of town. Neither was sure, later, which one suggested it, but they decided to take in dinner and a movie together. But first Susan wanted to go home and change clothes. John suggested he come by and pick her up. "After all, you're on the way to the theater, and there's no reason for both of us to drive." They dined, and again shared popcorn and enjoyed the movie. After the movie, John took Susan home and she asked, "Would you like to come in for a cup of coffee before you go home?" And John had that cup of coffee—with the breakfast that Susan fixed for him the next morning.

It all started with an innocent complement, but ended in adultery. At no time did either of them think about an affair, but it happened.

That's how it happened with me. The farthest thing in my mind was having an affair. But I was vulnerable because I lacked the attention and affection from my husband that another man was willing to give to me.

1 Corinthians 10:13 says, "No temptation has overtaken you but such as is common to man; and God is faithful, who will not allow you to be tempted beyond what you are able, but with the temptation will provide the way of escape also, that you may be able to endure it." The best means of escape is not allowing yourself to be put into a position of temptation.

Set hard, fast rules. Don't put yourself in a position of being alone with the opposite sex for any reason. Marsha and I won't go to dinner, or even ride alone with a member of the opposite sex other than a family member. This has sometimes posed challenges in the business world, in which case each of us makes sure the other knows exactly what we're doing and where we're going. We know from experience that an innocent event can lead to serious consequences.

MARSHA: It gives me a tremendous amount of strength knowing that Jim is praying the Lord's Prayer over himself, me, our marriage and our family. Jim also knows that every morning I am praying this for him. I pray first, "Kingdom of God come in my life," and then

"Kingdom of God come in his life." I pray the same prayer for our sons and their families.

Husbands, you are handing your wife so much security when she knows you pray this for yourself, for her and for your family. You have no idea what it will do to pray this prayer every morning.

It's not that I can't do anything wrong because I prayed the prayer, or because Jim prayed the prayer. We all stumble, of course, but I know that because of those prayers I can get back up when I do stumble.

JIM: *There are no magic formulas to a successful marriage. But there are kingdom principles that we can apply in order to experience a successful marriage. The first principle is for Jesus Christ to be the center of the marriage relationship. And the second principle is prayer.*

Our prayer is that those who learn from God's Blueprint for Marriage and already have a good marriage will have a better marriage as a result. And those who have struggles in their marriages will find their marriage better as a result of "God's Blueprint".

PART TWO

CHAPTER ONE
MARRIAGE IS A CROSS-CULTURAL MINISTRY!

Men and women are different! They are not just physically different. The way men think, the way women think, the way men react, the way women react, the way men respond, the way women respond...they are different.

Marriage is, in fact, a cross-cultural ministry. If you were going on the mission field in a foreign country, you would want to learn the language and culture of the people you would be serving. You would want to understand what makes them "tick". The same thing is true in marriage.

A husband cannot effectively "minister" to his wife until he learns how his wife thinks. He needs to learn to understand his wife the same way a missionary learns his mission field. He has to learn that she doesn't think the same way he does. Culturally, she is from a different world, and he has to learn to communicate with her in her world.

It's the same for a woman. She has to learn why her husband reacts the way he reacts,

why he thinks the way he thinks, and so on. This is how the two of them can live together in unity.

MARSHA: When Jim and I were first thinking about getting married, there were some things about him that I didn't like. I thought, "Boy, wait until we get married. Then I can really change him." It didn't happen. And if a woman goes into a marriage thinking that she can change her husband, she's wrong.

Or if the husband thinks he can change her, he's wrong. It isn't going to happen. We change by our own choice to fit into each other's lives, but we can't change each other. If a wife learns why her husband responds the way he does, she won't become frustrated herself—or frustrate him—by trying to change him.

JIM: *There are gender-based differences, temperament-based differences, personality-based differences, environmentally-based differences, and culturally-based differences. And each one of these differences raises the potential for communication problems. Marsha's and my differences affect the way that we communicate with each other.*

We want to look, first, at the gender-based

communication differences—those things that in general, men do because they are men, and women do because they are women. And, because men are men and women are women, there are misunderstandings that can occur as a result.

Most women would say, "My husband just doesn't understand." We want to learn why women don't understand men, and why men don't understand women. If we do, we can help husbands and wives communicate with each other.

CHAPTER TWO
MEN ARE HEADLINES; WOMEN ARE THE ARTICLE

MARSHA: Men are the headlines; women are the article. For example, I was a stay-at-home mom. When Jim came home from work, I might say, "Hi, honey, how was your day?"

JIM: *"Fine."*

That is a very common response of husbands to their wives. But if I asked Marsha, "How was your day sweetheart?" she might respond:

MARSHA: "Well, my day started when I first heard the boys. I covered my head up and shut my eyes hoping they would go back to sleep, but they didn't. Finally, I had to open my eyes and stretch, and I threw back the covers, and I twisted out of the bed and put my feet on the floor, put on my slippers, put on my robe, and I walked out the door..."

JIM: *This is the difference between a woman's and man's communication. Mine was an 8-hour time span. Marsha's was, too. Mine was eight hours at work; hers was eight hours at home with two boys. And my description of my day was one word, "Fine."*

As far as I'm concerned, "fine" was all that needed to be said. I had a good day. If I would have had a bad day, I would have said something like "Oh, it wasn't too good. It was kind of a bad day." And I wouldn't want to talk about it.

On the other hand, when she starts going into all these details, most men are thinking, "I really don't want that much information!" Be honest, guys You would just as soon she said, "Fine," and let it go at that.

But that won't happen, because most women are not made that way. They want to give you every detail of their day. So, here's what husbands need to do: Pay attention as though every word that she says is important to you! **Let her know that what she is saying to you is the most important thing you have heard all day.**

Men need to understand that she wants to hear what went on in your day beyond "fine." Men are not generally able to go into every little detail. We don't think that way. But you need to give her more of an answer than "fine."

MARSHA: For the stay-at-home mom, her vocabulary with kids has been "no", "yes",

55

"O.K.", "Pick up your toys", "Go to your room." Her opportunity for real communication is very limited. When her husband gets home she needs an outlet for conversation.

JIM: *A man needs to listen to his wife talk. It's the husband's responsibility to give her an outlet, especially if she is a stay-at-home mom. If you don't, I promise you she will explode sooner or later, and it isn't pretty when she does. Because she will explode all over you!*

MARSHA: Many times we wives learn second-hand what is going on in our husband's lives. If I want to know what is happening in Jim's life, I listen to his conversations with others. Eventually, I hear all about what is going on. It doesn't mean that he is a bad person or that I am a bad person; that's just the difference between us.

For example, Jim can be on the phone carrying on an extended conversation, and when he gets off the phone I will ask, "Who was that?"

JIM: *"Steven."*

MARSHA: "What did he have to say?"

JIM: *"Oh, not much."*

MARSHA: Or there have been times when Jim was going to a meeting, and I'd say, "Take the recorder." I want to be a part of his life. He has gotten better over the years. He knows when he gets home I am going to ask him what happened.

JIM: *I don't actually take a recorder, but sometimes I do take notes. I want to include her in my life, so I make myself pay attention to the details to share them with her. And, even though it is my nature to paint with broad strokes, I work to overcome that nature.*

MARSHA: Occasionally, we run into relationships where the roles are reversed. When the man comes home she says, "How was your day?" he tells her every detail. And when he asks how her day was, she says, "Fine." When the men are very detail-oriented, usually their wives are not.

JIM: *Men need to understand that our wives need details from us. Women need to understand that this is not comfortable for most men. It is a strain when they do, and it is a strain on their wives when they don't. Couples need to learn to adjust. You are not going to change your mate. That's the way he is--that's the way she is. It's the way God created us. Women, you have to be patient when the man says, "Fine." Men, you have to be patient when she wants details.*

Marsha had this perception that her dad would come home after work every day and sit down at the table while her mom prepared dinner. He would tell her mom every detail about his day. Because her dad and mom were Marsha's models for husbands and wives, she assumed that after I came home from work that I should sit down and tell her about every detail in my day. We resolved this one day when she said, "My dad always did...." I looked at her and said, "I am not your dad!"

MARSHA: The funny thing is, when we began developing *God's Blueprint for Marriage* I told Mom about remembering Dad sitting at the table telling her about his day. Mom said, "He never did that. He always came home and wanted to be left alone." He would come home and just say, "Fine." But, in my mind, I remember him sitting there.

Jim always needed a little bit of time when he came home to shift from work to home. The boys and I would not meet him at the door with, "Dad, I need your attention right now," stuff. Instead, we would give him time to change his clothes, sit down and relax, watch the news or whatever. Afterwards, we would bombard him with our day. That worked in our home. You have to find out what works in your home.

Couples should work at communicating any time they are together. After being apart all day, communication brings them back together. And communication is both talking and listening. Both need to talk and both need to listen.

CHAPTER THREE
COMPARTMENTALIZED AND MULTI-TASKING

JIM: *One reason men need time to unwind is we are compartmentalized. We don't multi-task. I focus on one thing at a time. I see one thing at a time. I can concentrate on one thing at a time. And if Marsha needs my attention, I can't just immediately drop what I am doing and shift my focus to her. I have to "close that window" and "open the next". Women, on the other hand, can see all sorts of things going on at the same time.*

MARSHA: I could watch TV, help Jeff with his homework, keep an eye on Mike out in the backyard, cook dinner, and talk on the phone all at the same time. I have no problem multi-tasking.

I never understood why most men would watch TV and had to hear every word that was spoken. If we were watching a DVD, and somebody walked in front of the TV, we would have to rewind because they missed something. I thought, "I can't understand this! What is wrong with these guys that they have to hear every single word? Or see every action?"

It drove me crazy. Our son could have run through the room screaming, bleeding to death, and if Jim were watching TV or reading a book I would think, "Did you not see this kid dripping blood?"

JIM: *"No, where?" I might have been oblivious.*

That's just the way it is. There are exceptions, but men generally can only see one thing at a time, while women can see lots of things at the same time.

CHAPTER FOUR
ANALYTICAL AND EMOTIONAL

MARSHA: Men are analytical; women are emotional. When we moved to Rogers, we were without a sofa. Every woman knows that a home needs a sofa. You need somewhere to lie down and watch TV, or when you have company, you need the seating. A living room is just not complete without a sofa. I needed a sofa!

JIM: *While I didn't disagree that a sofa would be nice, I knew we had four chairs in the living room, and four more chairs around the table in the dining room. We could seat eight people, and you couldn't get much more than that in our living room anyway. It would be nice to have a sofa. But it wasn't a necessity, and we did not have the money to buy one.*

MARSHA: So, I used "the hook". I told Jim, "I know we can't afford to buy one, but let's just go look." So we looked. We found the sofa I wanted, but did not buy it.

A few weeks later I saw in the paper the sofa I wanted was on close out. I thought, "I don't want to lose this sofa." So, I told Jim, "Let's go see if we can put it on layaway." So, that's what we did.

JIM: *We found a compromise. I knew we could not afford to go buy that sofa then, but she wanted the sofa yesterday. There was potential for conflict, because we were not in agreement. But we found ground for compromise. We put the sofa on layaway with $15 down! Then week by week we paid a little bit here, a little bit there. When extra money came in we put it toward the sofa, and finally we were able to bring it home.*

MARSHA: Yea! I had a sofa in my living room! And it looked good. It completed the room.

JIM: *Women think with their emotions. There was nothing logical that said we **had** to have a sofa. We had plenty of places to sit. And if you couldn't sit in one of the eight chairs immediately available, we had another chair in the guest bedroom and four metal folding chairs. We had plenty of seating.*

MARSHA: But we didn't have a sofa!

JIM: *We do now. But it is not because I gave in to her emotions, or because she gave in to my analysis. We found a place where we could agree. That's what makes marriages work--you don't each hold firm in your position. You come together and meet on common ground. Otherwise, it would be, "NO, you can't have a sofa!" Then her response would be, "Well, it's a good thing we don't have one because that's where you would be sleeping tonight."*

MARSHA: Most of the money that went on the sofa did not come directly out of our living expenses, but was extra money. And the balance that was due on the sofa was a gift to us. So I could say that it must have been God that we have a sofa, because He gave us the gift.

JIM: *And I could say, yes, it was God, because He knew we did not have the money to buy it. So He provided over and above what we needed. But we had to come to a common ground in order for God to work things out for us.*

CHAPTER FIVE
MEN SEE THE FOREST; WOMEN SEE THE TREES.

Jim: *Suppose we are planning a trip to Yellowstone National Park. I would get the map out, see where Yellowstone National Park is, and figure out how to get from here to Yellowstone. Then as far as I am concerned, I have done all the planning that is necessary; I know how to get there. Then, come the morning when we are to leave I would get up, throw some underwear, some socks and a couple extra pairs of shorts in a bag. Add my toothbrush and my razor and I am ready to go.*

Marsha: But I would have to start several weeks ahead for the trip. I would make a list of things that needed to be done. When the boys were young I had to make arrangements for someone to take care of them. It's not that Jim didn't think about that, or that it wasn't important. But he knew that I would take care of the details. I would make sure the house was clean, there was plenty of food and all the laundry was done before we leave.

When Jim came home, he would have gassed up the car and everything would be ready for him to load. He would remark how easy it was to get ready to go. Meanwhile, I would have been working for two weeks getting ready!

JIM: *And I would have done my part, figuring out where we are going and how to get there! Men see the end result, the big picture. Women see the details. That's why God gave women to men. The Bible says wives are helpmates. They complete us where we are deficient. I am not a list person, so what did God do? He gave me a list person. Sometimes the roles are reversed; if the husband is a list person, chances are he marries a woman who is not a list person. They complement each other.*

CHAPTER SIX
YOUR EAR, NOT YOUR HELP

JIM: *There is one issue that continually gets us men into trouble: We are quick to give our wives solutions to problems, when what they really want is a listening ear to help them sort things out. Men tend to be task-oriented. If Marsha came to me and said, "I've got a problem", My response would likely have been, "Well, it's real simple. All you have to do is A, B, C and it is fixed." But instead of accepting my solution, she would start crying.*

She doesn't want A, B, C. She wants me to listen to her about her problem. Wives want their husbands' understanding, not their solutions.

MARSHA: Sometimes, we just want our husbands to put their arms around us and say, "I understand; I am with you; we will work this thing out together," instead of, "Do this, this, and this and your problem is solved.

JIM: *Men just want to fix it.*

MARSHA: It's important for wives to understand why their husbands are quick to solve problems rather than be a sounding board while their wives sort things out. They are, by their nature, problem solvers. They need to help their wives solve their problems.

JIM: *Men would avoid a lot of conflicts if they quit trying to solve their wives' problems for them. That may not make sense to most men. We tend to think that when they come to us with a problem, they want us to solve it for them. And there should be no reason for conflict, because "I did the very thing that she asked me to do for her." Or so you thought.*

There are times when it is appropriate to tell her how to fix the problem, but it isn't when she first tells you about it. When your wife shares a problem that you think she wants you to fix, keep your mouth shut and your arms open. Let her work through the emotional side of the problem. Then give her your answer when she asks for it.

CHAPTER SEVEN
CHALLENGE AND SECURITY

Jim: *Men are motivated by challenge: attack and conquer!*

Marsha: Women are motivated by security.

Jim: *Can you imagine the conflict that Abram and Sarai might have had when Abram came home and said, "Honey pack up, we're moving," and she said, "Where?" and he said "I don't know. All I know is God said move. We're going to move." I can imagine what Marsha might have said.*

In September, 1996, we were asked to consider planting a church in Doris, a small northern California town. Before we left to check it out, I was sure we would be moving to California. There as an opportunity, a challenge. And I was ready to accept that challenge, take on Goliath and win that victory.

Upon arriving in Doris, we found the town was as poor as any town in the United States could be. Doris' primary industry was logging. But environmentalists had been responsible for shutting down the logging industry because of the threat to the spotted owl. As a result, most of the town's people were out of work. The number one source of income was welfare.

MARSHA: Housing options were sub-standard. I thought, "I am three days away from my family. We would be leaving the boys and my parents, and my dad was in poor health. There seemed to be no way that they would be able to come see us. And we wouldn't be making enough money to go see them.

I was thankful I did not feel God saying, "Yes, this is where you are supposed to move," because I didn't know that I could have handled it. Of course, I could have if God had wanted us there. But at the time I thought, "This is definitely not the place". Then I had to think, am I looking at it emotionally? Is this really where God wants us, and am I saying "No" out of emotion? It was pretty scary. And my security would have been jerked out from under me.

JIM: *And I was ready to go. But God did not give the both of us peace about moving. Had God said "Yes," He would have resolved all of those issues that Marsha was struggling with. He would have given her His peace if we were supposed to go. But she didn't have that peace. God showed us that moving to that town was not His plan for us.*

Logically, going there made no less sense than other moves we had made. When I went into full time ministry I took a two-thirds cut in pay. And when we moved to Rogers, Arkansas, we agreed to a guaranteed salary one-fifth of my salary in Tulsa.

But, in coming to Rogers, Marsha's security was not threatened because the move was right and God gave her peace about it.

When God gives direction, He will give both husband and wife confirmation. If the two of you do not agree, wait until you do before taking any action. There must be unity in your decisions that affect your family's security.

CHAPTER EIGHT
MICROWAVES AND SLO-COOKERS

JIM: *When it comes to romance, men are like microwave ovens. And for the most part, women are like slo-cookers. In an instant, men can be ready for an amorous time together.*

MARSHA: So much of our romantic mood depends on what goes on beforehand. We have to get "warmed up". We need to be romanced throughout the day. It's the little things, the call in the middle of the day to say, "Hi, I was thinking about you," the little pat on the butt, the kiss out of nowhere, a little note laying on the counter or on her desk at work. It's anything that makes us feel important to you.

JIM: *Guys, sex does not begin in the bedroom. It begins when the day begins. How you treat her during the day will determine how she responds to you later.*

MARSHA: We were counseling a couple that was having marriage problems. They have four children, and the wife couldn't understand why her husband would be sitting in the living room with shoes all over the floor. Their kids would come in and trip over the shoes; and he may have tripped over them as well. She couldn't understand why he didn't pick up the shoes. His comment was, "I didn't even see them." That incident is what sparked my understanding that there really is a difference between men and women.

The most important thing to remember from this section is, woman, you cannot change your man. God created him with his personality and with his the gender traits. You need to understand him and work with them to help you in your marriage.

JIM: *And we men have to learn to understand that our wives are the way God created them to be. Marriage truly is a cross-cultural ministry. We need to learn to understand each other's differences.*

.

PART THREE

CHAPTER ONE
THE NUMBER ONE PROBLEM IN
MARRIAGE: SELFISHNESS

Therefore be imitators of God, as beloved children; and walk in love, just as Christ also loved you, and gave Himself up for us, an offering and a sacrifice to God as a fragrant aroma....Wives, submit to your own husbands as to the Lord...Husbands, love your wives, just as Christ also loved the church and gave Himself up for her." (Ephesians 5:1-2, 22, 25)

MARSHA: Why do couples have marriage problems? The number one reason can be summed up in one word: **selfishness**. Selfish, self-centered living is the biggest reason people not only have marriage problems, but problems with other relationships as well.

Jim and I were trying to find a solution to our marriage problems, so we went to some counselors. I said to every one of them, "He makes me so mad because..." One counselor dropped a gold mine in my lap when he said, "He does not make you mad. Nobody can make you mad. It is a choice that you make."

When I am mad, Jim doesn't make me mad; I

choose it. It is a choice we make day by day by day, maybe even minute by minute.

JIM: *A man comes with three basic needs from his wife: to represent him well in public, to treat him well at home, and love him when he feels amorous. As long as those three needs are being met, he is basically satisfied.*

Most husbands think their wives were placed in their lives to fulfill his needs. And most wives think their husbands were placed in their lives to fulfill her needs. What he wants isn't happening; what she wants isn't happening. So they lock horns. Then they come to us for counseling.

For example, a wife told us, "My husband is not spiritual enough." I asked her, "What makes you think you are more spiritual than he is?" She said, "Because I pray all the time and he doesn't." She was spiritually arrogant in their relationship. She felt he wasn't meeting her spiritual needs because, in her mind, he wasn't praying enough. When I asked her about her husband's irresponsibility, she said he didn't take care of the bills, so she had to take over.

After we met with both of them, she realized he was much more spiritually mature than she thought. Her self-centeredness had clouded her vision, and it affected their entire relationship. Once her eyes were opened, her perception of his irresponsibility was resolved as well.

Selfishness manifests itself in so many ways. In the next chapter we will share how to overcome selfishness.

CHAPTER 2
SUBMISSION

MARSHA: One of the most difficult issues for women is submission, yet it is the number one key to a happy and successful marriage. Men love this subject.

JIM: *Yes, I like to read this Scripture to the men. "Wives,[I love this] "Submit to your husbands as to the Lord, for the husband is the head of the wife, as also Christ is the head of the church, and He is the Savior of the body. Therefore, just as the church is subject to Christ, so let the wives be subject to their own husbands in everything." (*Ephesians 5:22-24)

MARSHA: Submission is an attitude between two equals; obedience is an action between two un-equals. Husband and wife are on the same level; they are equal. But the one submits to the other. Obedience is between children and parents, the children are obedient to the parents because they are unequal.

The Amplified Bible reads:

"Wives, be subject, be submissive and adapt yourselves to your own husbands, as a service to the Lord. For the husband is head of the wife as Christ is head of the church, Himself the Savior of His body. For as the church is subject to Christ, so let wives also be subject in everything to their husbands. Husbands, love your wives as Christ loved the church and gave Himself up for her, so that he might sanctify her, having cleansed her by the washing of water with the Word, that he might present the church to himself in glorious splendor, without spot or wrinkle, or any such thing, that she might be holy and faultless. Even so, husbands should love their wives as their own bodies. He who loves his own wife loves himself. For no man ever hated his own flesh, but nourishes and carefully protects and cherishes it as Christ does the church, because we are members of his body. For this reason, a man shall leave his father and his mother and shall be joined to his wife and two shall become one flesh. This mystery is very great, but I speak concerning Christ and the church. However, let each man of you love his wife as his very own self, and let the wife see that she respects and reverences her husband, that she notices him, regards him, honors him, prefers him, venerates and esteems him, and that she defers to him, praises him, loves and admires him exceedingly." (Ephesians 5:22-33) [8]

The feminist movement of the 60's and 70's distorted the woman's image. We are equal with men, and that should be especially reflected in the workplace. But in the home, though we are equal with our husbands, we are to submit to them. Somebody has to be in charge. When I finally understood this, it was easy for me to relax in my role as a wife and submit to my husband. There is blessing that comes from the submission to the authority that God has placed over you, not just in marriage, but in all areas of life. Submission is not an ugly, dirty word.

When I first thought of submission, I thought, "doormat". Am I supposed to sit there and do whatever he wants? I thought, "I don't think so!" I could just see him, "Water please!" Or, "Slippers!" Or "Go fetch the paper!" That's for dogs! Submission is not slavery!

If you want to know what Scripture means, do a word study. The first word we are going to study is "submit". It is the same word as "subject". Vine's Expository Dictionary[9] says that it is primarily a military term that means to rank under, to put under, or be in subjection to. Webster's Online Dictionary[10] defines "submit" as to yield oneself to the authority or will of another, to yield oneself as a subject, to defer to the opinion or authority of another.

Webster says "subject" is one that is placed under authority or control. So Vines and Webster agree that you are under authority. It doesn't mean you are less; you are equal, but under the authority of your husband.

Respect, according to Webster, is to consider worthy of esteem; to regard with honor. That means respecting your husband is not just honoring him; you are to esteem him. It is to take notice of; to regard with special attention and to regard as worthy of special consideration[10.]

Reverence, in verse 33, says "However, let each man of you love his wife as his very own self and let each wife see that she respects and reverences her husband." Reverence is to fear--a reverential fear on the part of a wife for a husband. Webster describes it as proceeding from or expressing reverence, inspiring reverence.

The next word is notices him. That is to treat with attention. I have been visiting with several friends about submission. We agreed that our days become so routine that we sometimes don't even notice our husbands.

One friend shared about how she would come home after work and fix the evening meal.

Her husband would come in, walk through the kitchen past his wife to the bedroom, change his clothes then come out of the bedroom. She would never even acknowledge he was home...she didn't even notice him. But when she starting turning around and saying, "Hi, honey, how was your day," or something similar—when she started noticing him—their marriage changed. He still did the same thing when he got home, but he just did them a little differently. They would spend time when he first got home from work, just talking. He's a great talker, so that is what he needed.

Let the wife see that she respects and reverences her husband, that she notices him, regards him. Regard means look, gaze, the worth or estimation in which something is held, a feeling of respect and affection, to hold account, to pay attention to, to think of, to look attentively, to gaze, to pay attention, to heed. That's regard.

Honor him: one whose worth brings respect or praise, an exalted title or rank, respect and esteem shown to another. Honor may apply to recognition of one's title, to great respect or to any expression of one's recognition, implies a yielding.

Prefers him: to promote or advance to a rank

or position, to choose or esteem above another, to give priority. When our boys were little and we were putting our marriage back together they knew they were very, very important to us. They were the apple of our eye, so to speak, that we would do anything for them. But they also realized that, in my eyes, their dad came first, and in dad's eyes, mom came first.

Some advice my mom gave me before we married was to remember that your children are with you for a while and then they are gone. What you and your spouse do to maintain your relationship while raising your children is important. Because someday they are going to be gone. At that point you could be married to your best friend, or a stranger.

Everything you do should say something to your mate about how important he or she is to you. I know babies require a lot of attention and they require a lot of work, and husbands need to understand that babies need to be fed, changed and so on. But wives have to realize that there is a time and a place for her husband; he is very important to her, and he may not hang around until that baby is grown if he is not noticed, honored, preferred.

Venerate means to regard with reverential

respect or with admiration or deference. Esteems him: praise, regard, consider, to set a high value on.

Defer: to refer for a decision, to submit or yield to another's wish or opinion.

Praises him: to express a favorable judgment of, commend, to glorify, to express praise. A man's ego is a wonderful thing. Women, learn how to serve your man's ego. Learn what flips his skirt!

Sometimes I look at this and think, "What do you think he is...God?! Praise him, admire him?" No, that's not the case. But we need to praise our husbands for the work they do. It's not easy in the work place. Men are under a lot of pressure to make a living. The Scriptures are very specific about a man making a living for his wife and his family[11]. Even if the wife is the primary breadwinner, the husband still carries the weight of responsibility for his family. We need to praise our husbands; we need to be their cheerleader.

A friend once told me that I needed to be Jim's cheerleader. I'm not a cheerleader; that's not my character. My friend said to **learn** to cheer. Now, that's not a "Rah-Rah-

Rah!" type of cheerleader. It is encouraging him when he is down; it is praising him for a job well done. I probably don't thank Jim enough, but I thank God daily that I have a man that is willing to go every day and make a living for us. He's willing to do whatever it takes to support our family. We need to praise our husbands for their willingness to do that.

The scripture ends with, "loves and admires him exceedingly," which means extremely. In a day of "Xtremes", we need to be "Xtreme" in our demonstration of submission to our husbands. We need to understand that it is through our submission—through our yielding to our husbands—that the blessings of God come.

If I am not submitted to my husband I am stopping the flow of God's blessings. It's that simple. Many women don't understand the importance of submitting to their husbands as the authority God has placed in their homes. I didn't place Jim in the authority of our home; God placed him there. It's not his fault; it's not my fault. It's God's fault! But I am supposed to do my part. And if I don't, it builds a wall and stops the blessings.

I am not saying God can't get through that

wall. But you will not experience the fullness of His blessings until you learn to submit to the authority God places in your life, at home or in the workplace. Submission is a powerful word and through your submission comes unity in your marriage.

There have been times when I thought Jim was making a big mistake. But I didn't go to him and gripe and complain. I went to the Father and prayed, "Lord, if I'm wrong show me. If he's wrong show him." Before long Jim would say, "I'm sorry, I was wrong," or God would show me that Jim was right.

The best advice I can give women is, "Submit to your husbands (Ephesians 5:21)." Through submission come the blessings God has for you in your marriage, in your family, in your home, and in your life.

[8]Amplified Bible (The Lockman Foundation, Zondervan Publishing, 1965)
[9]Vine's Complete Expository Dictionary of Old and New Testament Words (W.E. Vine, Merrill F. Unger, William White Jr., Thomas Nelson,1996)
[10]http://www.websters-online-dictionary.org/definitions/respect

CHAPTER 3
GIVING UP

JIM: *Marsha has shared one side of the coin of Ephesians 5 as it relates to women. But there is another side of that same coin for men. If men think that everything Marsha shared about submission is intended to exalt them and make them "the king of the house", they are wrong!*

*Ephesians 5:1 says, "Therefore, be imitators of God as dear children and walk in love as Christ also has loved us and given himself up for us, an offering and a sacrifice to God for a sweet smelling aroma." Is there any doubt about Christ's love for us? Christ loved us so much that he was willing to die for us. It says, "Christ loved us and **gave himself up** for us." That's how you demonstrate love for someone—you give yourself up for them. That's how Christ loved the church. He gave himself up for the church.*

*In verse 25 Paul wrote, "Husbands, love your wives, just as Christ also loved the church and **gave himself up** for her." If you want to demonstrate that you truly are in love with your wife, that means **you give yourself up.** Jesus was saying, "I love you so much that I* *am going to give myself up for you and die for you." And Paul said that Christ expects us to do the same thing for our wives. What does that mean, to "give yourself up" for your wife?* **That means you submit to her.**

Now wait a minute. "If she is supposed to submit to me, then why do you think I should have to submit to her?" The answer is very simple: because the word of God says so. The true relationship between a husband and a wife is one of mutual submissiveness. I give myself up for her in the same manner that she is described as giving herself up for me.

Many men will take Ephesians 5:22, "Wives, submit yourselves to your husbands," out of context. They use that scripture to browbeat their wives into obedience. This attitude says, "I don't owe her anything, and she owes me everything." But in truth, that's not it at all. That's not submission; that's obedience. Stopping at Ephesians 5:22, and not continuing to verse 25 and giving ourselves up for our wives, does not demonstrate love for them. Rather, it demonstrates arrogance and selfishness. True love means giving yourself up…it means mutual submission.

Mutual submission does not mean that I acquiesce to her, but that I acknowledge to the world, and especially to her that, next to God, she is the most important person in my life. And because she is the most important person in my life, I am willing to give up those things that I thought were important.

I've heard some men say, "I'm married to her except during deer season. And during deer season she's a widow!" Hunting is more important than their wives. It's not that hunting in itself is wrong. But if hunting—or anything else for that matter—is at the expense of your wife, it is wrong.

What was important to me is no longer that important to me. What's important to me is what's important to her. I am willing to give up my own desires in order to help her fulfill her desires.

So here's what happens: Marsha is telling women, "Wives, submit yourself to your husbands." And I am to men, "Husbands, give yourselves up for your wives." The result is that we come together with an attitude of mutual submission.

What men have to realize is that God did not place you on this earth for your wives to serve you. God put you on this earth to serve your wives. Whether or not she ever serves you is irrelevant, because she was not given to you to serve you; she was given to you for you to serve.

Marsha: And, women, God did not place you on this earth for you to be served by your husband. God put you on this earth to serve your husband. Whether or not he ever serves you is irrelevant, because he was not given to you to serve you; he was given to you to serve him.

Jim: *The result is I that am busy serving Marsha, and she is busy serving me. My focus is not on me but her. And her focus is not on herself, but me. We are so busy meeting each other's needs there are no unmet needs. And even if there were, it wouldn't matter. "Even the Son of man did not come to be served, but to serve and to give his life a ransom for many" (Mark 10:25).*

MARSHA: When Jim was going his way and I was going mine, God told me to do one thing for him a day. I didn't even like him, and I thought, "Ugh! I have to do one nice thing." And I really had to think about what I could do for him every single day. But I would make sure his favorite shirt was ironed, or I'd make his favorite meal. I would send him a card; I would write something on the mirror in

90

lipstick— just something.

At first it was really hard because he did not respond. Once I stood in the doorway to our home office and watched him open a card I sent him. He read it and threw it away. I thought, "This isn't working. He is not even noticing what I am doing. He could care less if his favorite shirt is ironed or I made lemon meringue pie," or whatever. But eventually he did start responding and I would get a card, or a note lying on the counter. Or he would bring me flowers or call me during the day, which was a big step for Jim Dixon. Now we try to out serve each other every day.

JIM: I Peter 3:7 says, "In the same way you married men should live considerately with [your wives], with an intelligent recognition [of the marriage relation], honoring the woman as [physically] weaker but realizing that you are joint heirs of the grace (God's unmerited favor) of life, in order that your prayers may not be hindered and cut off."11

An intelligent man knows how to treat his wife. He also honors his wife, recognizing she is not spiritually or emotionally weaker.

If you are not treating your wife with the honor she deserves—if you are not esteeming her as you should—if you are not venerating her, your prayers will be hindered. If you are having problems with your prayers getting through, maybe you need to examine how you treat your wife. Esteem your wife; respect your wife.

MARSHA: The term, "weaker vessel" has been a sore spot for many women. I looked up the word "weaker vessel". That's what it means, weak, not as strong. Vessel is a container. So we are a weaker container. God did not make us to be **physically** equal with a man. Spiritually equal, physically weaker.   I don't want to change my own tire. If I have a flat, I am going to call my husband, and if he is not available, I'll call one of our sons. I am not going to get out there and change my tire. I'll walk!

I once heard a woman say, "Equality, I don't want equality. I don't want to have to lower myself to his level."

[11]Amplified Bible (The Lockman Foundation, Zondervan Publishing, 1965)

CHAPTER 4
SPIRITUAL HEADSHIP

JIM: *Husbands and wives are equal in their relationship with God and with each other. But there is an order of authority in the home established by the word of God. Men are to be the head of the house. In Ephesians 5:24 Paul writes, "Therefore just as the church is subject to Christ, so let the wives be subject to their own husbands in everything." To be subject to, or to be submitted to, does not mean to be dominated by or to be a doormat. But Marsha will tell you that once I took my place as the head of our home, she found a security that she did not have before.*

MARSHA: We just happened upon this principle. It wasn't a bolt of lightning that came down out of the sky and changed us. It was God working in us to establish the roles he wanted in our home. I draw a lot of strength and security knowing that, first, Jim hears from God. Second, he is obedient to what God tells him. He knows the word of God, so I can be secure in my role that God has for me in our home.

JIM: *"But pastor, you don't understand. My husband isn't worth submitting to! My husband's a jerk! He doesn't love the Lord!*

He's not willing to take his place in our home."
Wives, you may have a jerk for a husband, but
bad-mouthing won't make him improve. And,
unfortunately, badmouthing happens a lot. 1
Peter 3:2 says, "Wives, be submissive to your
own husbands that even if some do not obey
the word, they may be won by the conduct of
their wives, when they observe your chaste
conduct, accompanied by fear."[12] You can
submit to your husband to the point that he
becomes submitted to you. His observation of
your behavior is the witness he needs to come
to the realization of whom he should be in
Christ.

You are not going to change him by brow-
beating him. Proverbs 21:9 and 25:24 both
say, "It is better to live in a corner of the roof
than in a house shared with a contentious
woman."

Submit to your husband as the head of your
household, whether he acts like it or not.
Sooner or later, the Bible says, he will come
around as a result of your behavior. How long
*might that take? It might take years! **But***
***don't give up**.*

The same is true for husbands. If you have a
wife that you don't think is worth giving
yourself up for, she's still worth loving as

94

Christ loved the church. So love her anyway. We weren't worth loving either, yet Christ loved us enough that he was willing to give Himself up for us.

Headship does not mean domination, because the relationship between husband and wife is horizontal[13]. But the authority between husband and wife is vertical. You are equal in your relationship with God and with each other, but the wife should be under authority of her husband.

MARSHA: It is easy to know who the head of the house is. The hand that **controls** the finances rules the household.

Many years ago, I was taking care of the finances, juggling who we were going to pay and when. Finally, I had enough. I handed Jim the checkbook and said, "Here-it's yours!"

It was difficult for me to let go. I came from a home where, when the bill came, my dad would sit down, write the check, and the next day it went out. When Jim paid the bills, it was usually after late notices. A few times we even had our water turned off. But Jim realized they were serious about the bills being paid on time! But when I learned submission and headship and the authority

God placed in my life, I realized, "That is not my responsibility." Nowhere in the Bible does it say, "Men, write the checks." But the husband, as head of the home, should be responsible for the finances regardless of who actually pays the bills.

JIM: *That does not mean wives are not involved in financial decisions, or that they should live in blissful ignorance of the household financial condition. Nor do you dominate her by* **controlling** *finances. It's a case of financial responsibility.*

The bottom line is this: "Husbands, love your wives as Christ loved the church and gave himself up for her." Realize that you weren't placed on earth to have her meet your needs. You were placed on earth to meet her needs.

MARSHA: And, "Wives, submit to your husbands"—honor him, regard him, praise him, admire him exceedingly, like there is no other one on earth.

[12]New International Version (Biblica, Inc., 1984)
[13]Galations 3:26-28

PART
FOUR

Chapter One
Finances

We stated in a previous chapter that the number one problem in marriage is selfishness. The number two problem in marriage is finances. It is the husband's responsibility to be the provider of the household. I Timothy 5:8 says, "If anyone does not provide for his own and especially for those of his household, he has denied the faith and is worse than an unbeliever."

*Many families today are two-income families. That does not mean that the husband is an infidel, or that he is worse than an unbeliever. It just means that the circumstances are such that two incomes are required. But, who's **in charge** of provision? The Bible says it's the man. It does not say that he **delegates** that responsibility to her; it says that he **is** responsible for the finances. If he is not seeing personally to paying the bills, he is not really in charge of them.*

Many husbands don't even know where they are financially. They have abdicated their responsibility. In every case where we have done marriage counseling and the problem is finances, she paid the bills. She would say,

"But if I don't pay them, they won't get paid."
And our response was, "How do you know?"

MARSHA: I usually say, "So what?"! Jim
would wait until the cutoff notice came and
that was real hard for me. I remember
growing up that when a bill came it was paid
immediately. So, for me, waiting until the
cutoff notices arrived was difficult. But we
only had our electricity cut off two or three
times before Jim got the point. There were
times when I would call him and say, "Honey,
they are at the street cutting off our water,"
and he would say, "Oops!"

It would have been easy for me to take back
the financial responsibility. But I knew Jim
had to accept this responsibility as head of our
home.

JIM: *When a wife says, "If I don't pay it, it*
won't get paid," and takes over the finances,
she usurps her husband's responsibility and
hinders the flow of God's blessings.

Sometimes the husband abdicates his
responsibility, so wives feel it's necessary for
them to step in and take over. If the husband
were doing his part, she would not feel the
need to take over. Men have to accept their
responsibility. But sometimes wives have to

watch their husbands fail. The electricity won't be cut off more than once or twice before he gets the message!

MARSHA: God did not create women to handle the pressure of finances. Man was created to handle that kind of pressure. When we women take over the finances, we are taking it out of God's hands.

JIM: *I'll say it again; the one who makes the financial decisions is the head of the house. Sometimes the man abdicates his responsibility; sometimes she usurps. But in any case, whoever controls the finances controls the household.*

Sometimes different arrangements should be made within the family regarding who actually pays the bills. If he can't add two and two and come up with four, and she has a degree in accounting, it makes sense for her to balance the checkbook. It's a team operation, and the wife is involved in the process. But it is still his responsibility to decide what bills get paid and when, even if she makes the actual payment.

Being responsible for finances does not mean that the husband is the dictator of finances! Men should listen to wives, not only in finances, but in all things. Wives are the husbands' best source of counsel. God will speak to you through your wife. Sometimes when she says, "Honey, I think…" she might be saying what God has told her say, and you better listen.

The area of finances, particularly debt, is one of the devil's most effective tools against the believer. Debt is contrary to the will of God. Proverbs 22:26 (NKJ) says, "Do not be one of those who shakes hands in a pledge, or one of those who is surety for debts."

Debt is unsecured obligation. When the value of an item is greater than the indebtedness, or when you can sell it for more than you owe on it, it's not debt. If you can sell your house for more than you owe on it, the house is an asset. But when you owe more for something than it's worth, you are in debt. For example, most people are "upside down" in their cars. They owe more than the car is worth, and that is debt.

The devil uses instant gratification as a tool to put people in the bondage of debt. "I want it and I want it now. All I have to do is put it on the easy payment plan." That's "the lay awake plan." You lay awake at night worrying about how you are going to make the next *payment. That's what unsecured debt will do to you. It creates strife between you and your mate, because that financial obligation is always right in front of you. It gets between you, and you can't see each other for that debt.*

Some people's solution to debt is to max out their credit card and get another one! That's not a viable solution. We've known people who wanted to be in full-time ministry, but if the opportunity came up, they couldn't take it because they were in debt.

One couple we were counseling said, "But Jim, We have one card and we only use it for emergencies." I said "Oh, I get it, in God we trust, except in emergencies, and then we trust Discover!" The following week, when they came to our house, she said, "We cut up our credit card!"

Credit cards are not evil. The way to use credit cards and be a good steward is to pay them off on a monthly basis. "But you don't understand. I had extenuating circumstances." You think God didn't know that? God promises that He will supply all our needs. All He asks us to do is be faithful with what He has given us. Do what God says to do with what He gives you, and He will see that your needs are met. (Phil 4:19). If you will seek first the kingdom of God and His righteousness, He will meet your needs (Matthew 6:33).

*For those who have unsecured debt, our advice is to work to pay those debts off, **and stop using the credit cards!** In every financial counseling situation we've been involved in, unsecured debt was a factor. And our answer is always the same: "Cut up your credit cards and live within your means." To do otherwise stops God from being the provider He wants to be. God never intended for anybody to get into debt.*

CHAPTER TWO
THREE "S's"

Marsha: Women, if you don't remember anything else from this, remember three S's. The first "S" is **submit**. "Wives, submit yourselves to your husbands." (Eph 5:22). This point was thoroughly covered in a previous chapter.

The second "S" is **support**. I don't care what your husband's job is; you support him. During Jim's sales management career he would hire men who had great potential. But because their wives didn't support them, they quit. That irritated me, because instead of supporting their husbands, they were constantly discouraging them. No matter what he is doing, you be his cheerleader. Encourage him; let him know you are proud of him.

The final "S: is **shut up**! So many girls get on the phone and call mama or their best friend, and say, "You know what he did? He did blah, blah, blah." It is nobody's business but yours and your husband's.

It's nobody's business what goes on in the bedroom. The fight you had is nobody's business. If you really want to see me get angry, call me and criticize your husband. Ladies, you don't want your private lives to be locker room conversations. Respect your husbands enough to shut up! What goes on between you and your husbands stays just between you and husbands. Don't get on that phone and talk or get on the Internet and start chatting.

For example, let's say that I had a fight with Jim. I get on the phone and tell my mom, "You won't believe what my husband did." Then, he comes home and we make up. But my mom is still mad at him. She's holding a grudge, even though I have forgotten it. Then I call her up again and I say, "Boy, he is really being a jerk. I can't understand why he would . . ." And she takes up another offense even though Jim and I have worked things out. The offenses continue to build and build, and pretty soon she hates his guts because he's a no-good son-in-law who treats her little girl badly. It's so damaging. Don't talk to others about your personal problems. It's no one else's business.

JIM: There is an exception to the "Shut Up" rule. In the case of abuse—and both men and women can be guilty—this is not a time to remain silent. But choose wisely in whom you choose to confide. Talk to your pastor or a counselor—not your mom or your best friend—in the case of verbal or physical abuse or neglect. Abuse and neglect are not your fault, and certainly are not God's will for your marriage.

Physical abuse is a CRIME and should be dealt with as such. When I am asked (and generally by a woman) what to do under the circumstances, my response is, "Get away!" Marsha and I have taken several women to the local women's shelter in the past for physical abuse. Knowing their husbands/boyfriends are going to make every attempt to get her to return, and knowing that, statistically, an abused wife will leave an average of seven to eleven times before making it permanent[14], we tell her, "God loves you too much to want you in this situation," and will encourage her to get counseling as well as getting away. And, if appropriate, we will encourage the abused wife to report the abuse to the authorities and offer to go with her. Certainly, we discourage her from returning to the abusive husband until their counselors deem it safe to do so. Even then, the two of them should remain under close scrutiny.

[14]Helping Abused Victims: A Guide for Friends, Family, Classmates, & Co-workers (www.campbell.edu/pdf/counseling-services/helping-an-abused-friend.pdf)

CHAPTER THREE
FAMILY PRIORITIES

CHIDREN ARE FOR THE MOMENT; HE IS FOR A LIFETIME

MARSHA: We women can become so involved with raising our children, and so focused on them that we can neglect our husbands. But, some day those children will be on their own and raising their own families. While you are raising your children, you must choose whether you are going to be married to your best friend, or to a stranger, when your children are gone. Are you sending a message to your husband that the children are more important to you than he is? Be sensitive to the needs of your children. But make sure your husband knows how important he is to you.

JIM: *Marsha is talking about priorities. I heard Edwin Louis Cole say, at a men's conference, "Your priorities should be based on time of commitment. You are committed to God for all of eternity, so He should be your number one priority. You are committed to your mate for your life, so that should be your number two priority. Your children then, become number three." Then you can add in your career and other things that are important. If it is something that you are going to do for six weeks, how important is that in light of other priorities?*

MARSHA: One of my pet peeves is seeing moms in the back seats with their children rather than sitting in front with their husbands. Your place is next to your husband. If you need to tend to your child, pull over, tend to the need, and return to the front seat. When Jim and I were raising our boys, they sat in the back seat, and I sat in the front. My place was next to my husband, not next to my child in the back seat.

JIM: *Men, you need to date your wife. Set aside one evening a week for date night. If you are on a tight budget, go to McDonalds. Or take a walk in the park.*

Court her. Do things for her for no special reason. Stop on your way home and pick up a gift for her. It doesn't have to be expensive. Never stop treating her as special. There have been times when I didn't have money to buy Marsha a gift, so I wrote her a note. I think she has every note I ever gave her. And she cherishes all of them.

Remember, it's how you treat her outside the bedroom that determines how she will treat

109

you in the bedroom. There's an excellent book by Dr. Kevin Lehman, "Sex Begins in the Kitchen." It doesn't have anything to do with having sex in the kitchen! But it has everything to do with how you treat your wife throughout the day, because that will determine what kind of romantic life you will have.

Don't take her for granted. If she doesn't get the attention she needs from you she may find it someplace else. She can become very vulnerable, as we learned the hard way.

I've shared this secret with you already: "Husbands, love your wives as Christ loved the church and gave himself up for her. [15] *Give yourself up for your wife. Gals, give yourself up for your husbands.*

[15]Ephesians 5:25

CHAPTER FOUR
THE MARRIAGE COVENANT

There's a difference between a contract and a covenant. A contract is based upon mistrust, spells out specific terms in writing and, once signed and filed, is binding in the eyes of the law. It defines limited liabilities and can be voided by mutual consent or court decree.

A covenant is based upon trust and commitment between parties and is binding in the eyes of God. It requires unlimited responsibilities and liabilities, and cannot be voided by mutual consent or court decree.

When you marry, a certificate of marriage is filed at the county courthouse and although this has many of the characteristics of a contract, you aren't entering into a contract, you are entering into a marriage covenant. Some states, in fact, offer the option of a covenant marriage certificate.

The relationship between husband and wife is to be a reflection of the relationship between Christ and His bride, the Church. Husbands are to love their wives in the same way that Christ loves the church, giving Himself up for her. And, wives are to submit to their husbands in the same way the Church is to submit to Christ. It is mutual submission, as you give yourselves up for each other.

It is a great responsibility, being a reflection of the relationship between Christ and His bride. It's a responsibility that cannot be fulfilled alone. The Bible tells us, in Ecclesiastes 4:9-12:

9Two are better off than one, because together they can work more effectively.
10 If one of them falls down, the other can help him up. But if someone is alone and falls, it's just too bad, because there is no one to help him.
11 If it is cold, two can sleep together and stay warm, but how can you keep warm by yourself?
12 Two people can resist an attack that would defeat one person alone. A rope made of three cords is hard to break.[16]

Two are better than one, and three is better than two. It is the husband and wife, PLUS JESUS, that form the cord that is not quickly broken. Husbands and wives should nurture one another, and allow the Lord to nurture them. Relationship with Jesus should not be a once-a-week, only on Sunday thing, but a daily part of your lives.

Husband plus wife plus Jesus are an undefeatable team…a rope made of three cords. I challenge you to take on the world, as you live your lives together!

[16] My thanks to Pastor Phil Stern, who uses this description of covenant in his wedding ceremonies.
[17]Good News Translation (American Bible Society, 1976)

Made in the USA
San Bernardino, CA
27 May 2018